Evergreen Ape

The STORY of BIGFOOT

DAVID NORMAN LEWIS

Microcosm Publishing
Portland, OR

EVERGREEN APE
The Story of Bigfoot

© David Norman Lewis, 2021
This edition © Microcosm Publishing, 2021
First edition, first published September 9, 2021

For a catalog, write or visit:
Microcosm Publishing
2752 N Williams Ave.
Portland, OR 97227
www.Microcosm.Pub

ISBN 9781621065470
This is Microcosm #566
Edited by Sarah Koch

Design by Joe Biel

To join the ranks of high-class stores that feature Microcosm titles, talk to your local rep: In the U.S. **Como** (Atlantic), **Fujii** (Midwest), **Travelers West** (Pacific), **Manda/UTP** in Canada, **Turnaround** in Europe, **New South** in Australia and New Zealand, and **Global Publisher Services** in **Asia, India, South America,** and **South Africa**. We are sold in the gift market by **Faire**.

Global labor conditions are bad, and our roots in industrial Cleveland in the 70s and 80s made us appreciate the need to treat workers right. Therefore, our books are MADE IN THE USA.

Did you know that you can buy our books directly from us at sliding scale rates? Support a small, independent publisher and pay less than Amazon's price at www.Microcosm.Pub

Library of Congress Cataloging-in-Publication Data

Names: Lewis, David Norman, author.
Title: Evergreen ape : the story of bigfoot / David Norman Lewis.
Description: Portland, Oregon : Microcosm Publishing, 2021. | Summary: "The
  Pacific Northwest has always been home to unusual folktales, bizarre
  legends, and strange goings ons. From the countless UFO sightings and
  the dense rainforests of Oregon and Washington, to the sprawling network
  of Shanghai tunnels interlaced beneath the cities, the region is rife
  with stories of the unexplained and the unnatural. In Evergreen Ape,
  David Lewis takes a closer look at the origins of the Pacific
  Northwest's most beloved and elusive cryptid: Bigfoot. Drawing from
  newspaper reports, local American Indian legends, and stories passed
  down from settlers in the 1800s, Lewis explores the true stories that
  created the modern monster. Discover the various manifestations of the
  legend and the way he has interacted with society, then read about
  popular hikes in the area where he has supposedly been spotted, and step
  onto the path of finding Bigfoot yourself"-- Provided by publisher.
Identifiers: LCCN 2021019728 | ISBN 9781621065470 (trade paperback)
Subjects: LCSH: Sasquatch--Northwest, Pacific. | Northwest,
  Pacific--Folklore.
Classification: LCC QL89.2.S2 L48 2021 | DDC 001.944--dc23
LC record available at https://lccn.loc.gov/2021019728

MICROCOSM · PUBLISHING

Microcosm Publishing is Portland's most diversified publishing house and distributor with a focus on the colorful, authentic, and empowering. Our books and zines have put your power in your hands since 1996, equipping readers to make positive changes in their lives and in the world around them. Microcosm emphasizes skill-building, showing hidden histories, and fostering creativity through challenging conventional publishing wisdom with books and bookettes about DIY skills, food, bicycling, gender, self-care, and social justice. What was once a distro and record label was started by Joe Biel in his bedroom and has become among the oldest independent publishing houses in Portland, OR. We are a politically moderate, centrist publisher in a world that has inched to the right for the past 80 years.

Did you know that you can buy our books directly from us at sliding scale rates? Support a small, independent publisher and pay less than Amazon's price at **www.Microcosm.Pub**

CONTENTS

Bigfoot 7

Wild Men 13

Ape Canyon 35

Kings and Apes 51

Rousseau and Dahinden 69

Cripple Foot 79

Bigfoot Convention 95

Real Seattle Apes 105

A Bigfoot Hiking Guide 113

BIGFOOT

"He who seeketh long enough and hard enough will find the truth, whatever that truth may be."

–Roger Patterson, Bigfoot Hunter

Recently at a Seattle junk store, I found hundreds of unopened packs of *Harry and the Hendersons* trading cards. They are not collectables; they are worth less now than when the film first came out in 1987. Even though they still have the gum in them, people no longer care about Seattle's top family-friendly Bigfoot movie. "Wow, can you imagine kids used to trade these in school?" I asked a friend who was with me.

"Something tells me they didn't," he responded, "but I know what you mean."

There has yet to be a truly incredible Bigfoot movie.

At Seattle's Scarecrow Video, America's largest surviving video rental store, there is an entire Bigfoot movie section. Although it probably contains every Bigfoot movie ever made, just by looking at the covers it is clear that somebody will find Bigfoot before anybody makes a watchable movie about them. Be it *Harry and the Hendersons*, where Bigfoot brings a family closer together, or *Big and Hairy*, where Bigfoot plays basketball, or *Bigfoot vs. D.B. Cooper*, where Bigfoot constantly stares at buff, shirtless men, none of the available movies get at the essence of Bigfoot.

Bigfoot is hard to dramatize because he doesn't do anything. Aliens abduct farmers, vampires suck blood, the chupacabra sucks goat blood, the Mongolian Death Worm electrocutes people, but all Bigfoot does is exist, and existing is all he has to do for people to devote their lives to looking for him.

Why the idea of an undiscovered species of ape living in the Northwest wilderness is appealing to so many people is a bigger mystery than whether or not the creature exists. Dr. Grover Krantz—the professor of anthropology at Washington State University who nearly destroyed his career and lost countless promotions for his belief in Bigfoot—wrote that, even if a Bigfoot was ever found, "Life will go on, almost as if nothing had happened." Still, he was obsessed.

To a non-believer, most Bigfoot books are unreadably boring since they are usually just collections of people claiming to have seen one.

Yet people cannot get enough of them. My editor told me it is almost impossible for a Bigfoot book to lose money. Many booksellers have confirmed that people come into their stores and ask "do you have anything else on Bigfoot?" looking to read anything that might have a novel blurry photo of the elusive creature.

This was not always the case. Although stories of "Wild Men" are found in every culture on Earth, from Europe, Australia, and Japan, to Africa and North America, they did not capture the imagination of white America until the 1920s, and they did not become a mania until after World War II. According to the stories of countless American Indians, they have been around forever, yet during the 1924 "Ape Canyon" incident, there was not yet an English word to describe them, as Bigfoot and Sasquatch had never appeared in print.

As a social phenomenon, interest in Bigfoot is often attributed to a desire to "reconnect with nature," which explains why he was so popular during the hippie movement of the 60s and '70s. While this is partially true, it raises even more complicated questions: What is "nature"? How do you "reconnect" with it? Why do people want to "reconnect" with it to begin with? And, even more intriguing, why are the people with this desire almost entirely white?

In the decade leading up to the first famous modern Bigfoot sighting in the Northwest, the "Ape Canyon" incident of 1924, there were a variety of stories about the failure of man to connect with nature on the West Coast. While most of these stories are forgotten now, they provide a lot of insight into why the idea of Bigfoot was so popular. It was not until it was clear that man is incapable of perfectly merging with the natural world that the need for a man-ape to fill this void arose. No story from the early 20th century Northwest illustrates this better than the story of John Tornow. . .

WILD MEN

A September night. 1911. Rural Washington. Mrs. Bauer lay in bed beside her husband, unable to sleep. Earlier that day her twin boys had gone off to shoot a bear prowling around the cow pasture. They never came home. People all up and down the Satsop river had heard the gunshots coming from the pasture and later found the dead bear, but the boys had vanished.

While Mrs. Bauer laid in the dark worrying about them, she could hear the sound of something scrounging around in the kitchen. Without getting out of bed, she knew it wasn't the twins—it was the Wild Man.

In 1911, no whites had ever heard of apemen living in the Northwest woods. The word "Bigfoot" would not exist until the 1950s, and even the word "Sasquatch" would not appear in print until 1929. The Wild Man in Mrs. Bauer's kitchen was not some lost link between man and ape; it was her own feral brother, John Tornow.

Although she hadn't seen him since he escaped from the insane asylum down in Salem, Oregon two years earlier, she still knew it was him in the kitchen. In the two years since he broke out, Tornow frequently raided her house whenever he needed supplies that he couldn't get from the woods; matches, flour, thread, etc. He only came at night and Mrs. Bauer never confronted him or told her husband about the visits.

While apemen were not yet known of, there were reports from all over the West Coast that white men could go feral in the woods and transform into hairy monster giants. In 1914, following reports of a hairy giant in the woods of southern

Oregon, a reporter for the *Daily Capital Journal* wrote, "What a white man will do or will not do is one of the things that is not only beyond finding out but is without the pale of guesswork."

Mrs. Bauer did not know if her brother had grown animal-like hair all over his body like the men in the newspaper stories, but she did know the two most important things about him: one, he was insane, and two, he was the most lethal shot on the Olympic Peninsula. From the age of twelve, he'd been blasting snuff tins right through the center from a hundred yards away.

After escaping from the insane asylum in Oregon, he walked all the way back to the Olympic Peninsula on foot.

On arriving back in his home territory, he bought a shoebox full of ammunition at the general store and then asked a fur trapper to deliver a message to his family. He wanted his brothers and his sister to all know that he never planned on living indoors again. If any of them, or any strangers, tried to take him out of the woods, he would kill them. "These are my woods. I want to be alone."

Most people making a threat like that would have been tracked down and killed on sight, but the Tornow family was wealthy and influential on the peninsula. Tornow's deceased parents had even left $1,700 in the bank for him (the equivalent of $46,026.69 in 2020) and the deed to a chunk of the family land, in case he ever became tame and decided to leave the woods.

The locals did their best to give John Tornow his space, and tolerate him as a local character.

By the age of thirty-one, he had favored living out in the wilderness and sleeping on piles of moss and ferns. He told his parents that while in the woods he heard music "like that of organs and harps." At the time, there were plenty of people who felt similar to Tornow but did not take their love of the outdoors to the same extremes that would cost Tornow his life and lead to the death of at least six other people.

In 1889, the great American conservationist and co-founder of the Sierra Club, John Muir, visited the Olympic Peninsula. At the time of Muir's visit, Tornow was nine and would not be entranced by the woods for another year. Although Muir didn't meet Tornow, he reported "in these Washington wilds, living alone, all sorts of men may perchance be found—poets, philosophers, and even full-blown transcendentalists, though you may go far to find them."

The desire of the "full-blown transcendentalists" to meld with nature is *firmly* a white thing. The historian David Buerge has succinctly described Puget Sound Indian philosophy as "almost anti-transcendentalist." Although you could find plenty of crazy white people deep in the forests of the peninsula, one thing traditionally you wouldn't have found there was American Indians. The Native people of the Washington coast lived off of fish and hardly ever ventured into the woods, believing nothing awaited them there but death and insanity. As the author Murray Morgan wrote in *The Last Wilderness*: "In the legends of the coastal tribes the man who went into the forest was not called 'Brave Hunter' or 'Elk-Stalker' or anything like that; he was called simply 'The Fool.'"

When the industrial revolution brought psychotic white men to the peninsula—who wanted to get "back in touch" with a kind of nature they only knew from articles written by real estate promoters—the Natives of the coast knew it would end in disaster.

In the early 1920s, a Quinault elder named Bob Pope, who was born way before birth certificates but was at least ninety years old, told anthropologist Ronald Olson a legend about these white men who sought after an indifferent nature to love them.

According to Pope, there was once a white philosopher living alone on the Hoh river who had an ape-woman climb into his bed late one night. They had some spectacular Sasquatch-sex (technically "Siatko-sex" in Lushootseed, since Sasquatch is an anglicized Halkomelem word from Vancouver Island), finally fulfilling the white man's desire to become part of nature.

Right at the moment of climax, the white man died. The ape-woman died shortly after. The desire to merge the non-human world with civilization destroyed them both.

In the same way, whites who want to "get away from it all" and live in the woods wind up destroying the natural environment.

Walden Pond, which inspired the American transcendentalist Henry David Thoreau's *Walden; or, Life in the Woods*, is now so filled with human urine from swimmers that it is killing all the fish.

Mrs. Bauer had no romantic notions of nature, considering it had turned her brother into the monster in her kitchen. Blood the same as hers, but with a mind like a bear's. While most nights she would have just laid in bed and let John Tornow loot and leave, with the twins missing she had to talk to him.

Without even lighting a candle she entered the kitchen where her brother was filling his gunny sack. Tornow's clothing was always stuffed with fir needles for insulation, and the smell of fir filled the kitchen. "Johnnie. . . where are the boys?" Her voice startled him and he turned to leave. "They went after a bear yesterday afternoon when one of the cows went missing and they didn't come home. Did you see them?"

"I didn't know it was them when I shot."

Earlier that afternoon he'd been poaching one of his sister's cows when he'd been startled by his nephews' rifle shots. He didn't see the bear and thought they were after him. "I thought someone was shooting at me." He closed up his bag and looked at his sister without apologizing or explicitly confessing to anything. For the next eighteen months Tornow's sister would be the last person to ever see him and live.

He walked out into the moonlight. Mrs. Bauer's twins, in their symmetrical suspenders, were out there in the dark, buried under a mound of moss and leaves. Their arms had been crossed and their eyelids closed by the Wild Man himself. They could finally be told apart as one had a single bullet hole through the heart and the other had been shot twice, once in the stomach and once through the shoulder.

At the time, if any Puget Sound Natives had heard twins were involved they would have instantly realized this was going to be a story where the world of man and nature would become monstrously twisted. Giving birth in a litter was something animals did, not people. In Indian legends the birth of twins always marks impending disaster.

The Twana word for twins literally means "wolves," and the Twana elder Henry Allen described the revulsion his people felt for them by saying, "Bearing twins is not human, it is like animals!" There was a strict taboo on premenopausal women eating deer meat, since the cleft in the hoof reminded them of twins—horrible, subhuman, animal-man twins.

In 1911, the same year John Tornow started what would become a killing spree in order to remain in the wild, down the coast in California the last "Wild Indian" in North America, Ishi, finally came out of the woods, starved nearly to death, wearing a poncho made from the canvas of an old covered wagon. He was taken to a museum in San Francisco where he lived for the remainder of his life, sparking a debate about whether or not he should be returned to the wild.

Letters poured in from whites, who'd never met Ishi, arguing on both sides of the debate. Some thought he should be kept in the museum, writing it would be "cruel as cruel to turn that poor fellow loose." While others wrote that he should be set free as "It would be too bad if one of his childlike nature should be treated as one of ourselves."

What none of them knew was that Ishi had zero desire to ever leave San Francisco, or his museum. He'd gotten a job as a museum janitor and was saving up half his money, hoping to buy a horse someday.

The well-meaning whites had him confused with the whale from *Free Willy* in their belief that he had a natural craving to return to the wild. Ishi was not from the wilderness; he was from a tribe. Now that his entire family was dead he had nobody in the woods to return to.

In a less screwed-up culture, the natural habitat for a human is surrounded by other humans. On seeing the Pacific Ocean for the first time, Ishi was not impressed by the massive waves but was impressed by the massive amount of people on the beach, exclaiming "Hansi saltu! Hansi saltu!" Meaning, "So many white people! So many white people!"

On attending a vaudeville show, he spent the entire time watching the audience, and after the show it was the only thing he wanted to talk about. Cars did not interest him, but he found trolleys fascinating, as they fit more people. Ishi's preference for trolleys is one of the stranger endorsements for public transportation.

When Ishi's new white friends at the museum prodded him to go on a camping trip with them in the woods, he always refused. In a broken mix of English and his native language of Yana, he tried to explain to them that in the woods there was no electricity, no feather beds, no ice cream, no trolleys. After much begging from the whites, Ishi finally agreed to go with them, but assured them they would have a terrible time.

By the end of the trip the whites wanted to stay longer, but Ishi was the first to pack up their camp and get on the train back to San Francisco.

The Puget Sound anthropologist T.T. Waterman worked with Ishi and considered him to be the best friend he ever had, as did many of the other museum staff who came to know him, and many even tried to learn his language.

Although Ishi learned to like life in a white city, he had no immunity to white diseases and perished within five years of coming out of the woods in his covered wagon poncho.

Tornow and Ishi were both popular news stories in 1911 because they both represented the end of the frontier and wild America. Even decades later, in the mid-1940s, the historian Stewart H. Holbrook wrote that whenever the "Barrel-stove historians of the logging camps" told stories about Tornow they always brought listeners back to the "smoke haze of settlers' clearing fires" and "the toot and stutter of a logger's donkey engine."

Visiting the Satsop River country even now evokes the story of John Tornow, with its pockets of wilderness cut up by squares of cultivated farmland. The small-town reporter Hollis B. Fultz, author of *Famous Northwest Manhunts and Murder Mysteries*, was on the Satsop River the day the Bauer twins disappeared and he heard the sound of the gunshots coming from the cow pasture.

According to Fultz, the reason that things like bears, cougars, and John Tornow were stalking around ranches for food was because by 1911 there was not much game left in the ever dwindling woods.

Nobody knows how many people Turnow killed, but Fultz estimated that it was at least eleven. Most just vanished into the woods never to be seen again. His six confirmed victims are all recorded on a small bronze plaque at the Grays Harbor County Courthouse.

During the winter snow Tornow made no tracks. There were rumors that he got around the woods by swinging from branch to branch like an ape. A Swedish logger, Emil Swanson, came into camp shaking one night, "By Jesus I work here no more." Out in the woods he'd seen "some kind big animal look like man," swinging around above him in the night. To younger generations not around during the time of the murders, Tornow took on the role of a real Northwest superhero. When the historian Stewart Hall Holbrook interviewed young loggers in the 1940s he said they talked about Tornow "like a mix of Tarzan and Superman."

Tornow spent part of the winter living beneath the floorboards of a one-room schoolhouse like a possum. It was here that he saw his face on a "$1,000 Dead or Alive" poster and blasted the sign away with his rifle.

He then lived inside the rotted core of a gigantic dead cedar, known to fishermen as "The Big Tree on the Satsop." A game warden and a deputy sheriff were sent to kill him, only to be found with bullet holes straight through their foreheads. Tornow was indeed a good shot. He then buried them so their bodies formed the shape of a capital "T." T for Tornow.

Deputy Quimbly, a Spanish-American War veteran, received reports that Tornow had been spotted near the Oxbow River, and headed out with two fur trappers to kill him. When they reached the general area, they split up—the fur trappers coming at his hideout from one direction, Deputy Quimbly coming at him from the other.

While sneaking through the woods, Deputy Quimbly heard the sound of rifle fire. The trappers had found Tornow. The sound of rifle fire ended. During the Spanish-American War, Deputy Quimbly had been in combat five times. None of those battles were as scary as the silence which followed the rifle fire in the Washington wilderness. There was no shout of "We got him!" or "You around Quimbly?" The quiet made it clear who had won.

Deputy Quimbly hid down in the brush as he saw the shape of Tornow's back behind a hemlock tree. The Wild Man turned around. His hair was thick, tangled, and bug-infested. His fingernails had grown into claws, and yet the flesh on his face was white and smooth as a baby's. Tornow was nocturnal, he had not been in sunlight for years. It was the face of death. Deputy Quimbly knew he had only one shot before Tornow killed him. He fired. Tornow fell back, landing behind the tree.

The deputy's hand was shaking so bad he couldn't even hold the bullet while trying to reload. Without checking to make sure Tornow was dead, Quimbly ran back to town, never looking over his shoulder to see if anything was chasing, or swinging, after him.

In town, the deputy alerted the sheriff who assembled a posse big enough for a presidential safari. They ran back to the site of the standoff where they found the bodies of the fur trappers, but Tornow had vanished. Nothing around but moss.

Then came a shout; "Here's the son of a bitch." He lay beside the hemlock. In death he so blended in with the forest that he was almost invisible. On his feet were the shoes of a fisherman who had vanished on the Satsop a month earlier. Tornow's coat belonged to the deputy who'd tried to track him with the help of a game warden. In the coat's pocket was the game warden's bottle of strychnine; they'd planned on killing him by poisoning his meat, in the same way that ranchers killed off wolves stalking their herds.

The posse wrapped his body in canvas and propped him up in the passenger seat of a Model-T Ford, driving back to town. On the rocky dirt road his head bobbed the entire way. As his family was well respected in the area, he was taken to the undertaker.

The undertaker had never seen a body like this before; Tornow was nothing but bone and muscle. According to the undertaker his shoulders were like those of a gorilla, and the palms of his hands were like leather, giving some proof to the theory that he got around by swinging from branches. People from all over the peninsula came to see the body.

To rural Washington, he was not a serial killer. He was not a mental patient. He was "The Outlaw." Not like an outlaw who robbed banks; he was "The Outlaw" because he lived his life outside of all human laws—legal and social.

In the end his family buried him in the family graveyard, but with no inscription on his grave, hoping in time his story would be forgotten. Eventually some of his fans erected a proper tombstone: JOHN TORNOW: FROM LONER - TO OUTCAST - TO FUGITIVE. Eerily, the headstone depicts the Bauer twins stalking a bear across a deforested landscape, unaware they are about to be killed by their own uncle.

During the entire nineteenth century there were only a handful of big ape sightings in all of North America, but these were usually believed to be *white men* who had turned feral in the wilderness. When the *San Francisco Chronicle* reported on a gorilla-like creature in 1873 that was "covered all over with long black hair and had long gray whiskers," which was spotted picking berries in Squaw Valley, the paper added "He is a white man," despite nothing in the description sounding even remotely human.

This was also the case with the Dover, New Jersey Wild Man of 1894, the Lebanon, Oregon Wild Man of the 1880s, the Nevada Wild Man of the 1860s, and more. Despite describing these creatures as enormously tall, with inhumanly shaggy hair, it was believed that underneath that hair was still white skin.

Reflecting the pioneer's view of nature in general, it was believed that these Wild Men could be captured, tamed, and made into white men again. When the Lebanon, Oregon ape of the 1880s was seen chewing on the carcass of a dead deer, it was believed to be a man named John Mackentire who had vanished years earlier. A search party set out to capture and shave him, without success.

Revealing a white man underneath the fur of a gorilla typifies the frontier philosophy that even the most inhospitable terrain could be made into a fertile farm.

John Tornow was the closest a white man ever came to actually living like an animal, and his body being dragged before the townspeople and propped up like a trophy showed that it is impossible to truly escape civilization.

In the years immediately following his death there were some much tamer man-wild-merge stories that were popular in the Northwest, but all of these were by mostly rational men who wanted to challenge themselves to get back in touch with nature.

In 1914, "Nature Man" Joe Knowles arrived in Oregon from the East Coast, vowing to survive in the Siskiyou Mountains with nothing but a thong and his wits to protect him. He'd done it once before in Maine after having a prophetic dream. "Not much of a dream, but a damned real one," Knowles said. "I dreamt I was lost in the woods, alone and *naked*, with no hope ever of getting out. When I woke up I got to thinking if and how a civilized man should get along in such a situation."

On entering the Maine woods he wore only a thong, and months later came out dressed in Robinson Crusoe-type clothes he'd cobbled together himself. "My only regret at the time is that I didn't manage to catch a cub bear alive. I thought it would be a fine idea to come out of the woods leading a small and tamed bear behind me on a leash of willow."

Naturally, people accused him of faking it, so he came to the Northwest to do it again. The Hearst papers hired the anthropologist T.T. Waterman to referee the whole thing and make sure it was legitimate. T.T. Waterman, who had worked closely with Ishi and was the first white to ever speak to him in Yana, could honestly say that he was the only human in history who'd met both a man who'd come *out of* the wilderness almost completely naked, in need of food, and a man who went *into* the wilderness almost completely naked, in need of publicity.

Just weeks after Joe Knowles entered the Siskiyou Mountains, World War I broke out in Europe and the public lost what little interest they had in the "Nature Man." However, in the months after he gave up, a headline in *The Evening Herald* reported on further strange-doings in the Oregon woods "DEER HUNTERS SEE WILD MAN - SIX FEET TALL, NAKED, LAUGHING LIKE A FIEND, BEARDED WILD MAN FRIGHTENS TOWN OF LELAND." The creature was first mistaken for a cougar, but according to a deer hunter named Scotty, it would walk erect or drop on all fours at will. He was going to shoot but "this nature man let out such a continuous peal of demoniac laughter" that Scotty lost his nerve and the thing ran off. The paper remarked, "Maybe Joe Knowles is again growing a bunch of whiskers in the Oregon woods—who knows?"

Considering that Knowles could quit whenever he wanted, it was innately not as exciting as the story of Tornow's fight to the death to live like an animal. Knowles wound up spending the rest of his life living as a hermit on the Washington Coast near the town of Seaview. Until his death in 1941 he lived in a cabin completely made from materials salvaged from shipwrecks. To the very end he was bitter that he'd never been able to become one-with-nature the way he wanted. He would not answer any letters about his "Nature Man" days and wanted nothing else from the world except to be forgotten.

Outside his cabin on the Pacific Ocean he hung a sign on the gate which offered his final advice: "Stranger, Pause a While, Joe Knowles."

Ishi, John Tornow, and the lackluster Joe Knowles all vanished from the American consciousness in the following decades. The three of them had shown that the idea of a "Wild Man" was a contradiction.

Even if they had shown that it is impossible for a man to be wild, the desire to be wild would continue to increase in the following century.

It was the perfect breeding ground for the Northwest's greatest, biggest, most famous ape.

APE CANYON

*A*July morning. 1924. Seattle. It was the richest summer on record. Seattle had cars now, Seattle had radios, movie theaters, heated swimming pools, phonographs, dance halls, and airplanes. Barely over ten years and a hundred miles from the Tornow murders it was like a completely different country and century.

Even with all these new gadgets and conveniences, in July of 1924 the most talked about story in town were the ape monsters spotted on Mount St. Helens. Front-page headlines from *The Seattle Times* to *The Portland Oregonian* spoke of "Gorilla Men" and "Mountain Devils" and "Animals, Half Cougar and Half Ape." It was the first of the modern Bigfoot sightings.

Part of the reason the story caught on was because *The Seattle Times* already had a correspondent at Mount St. Helens to cover the arrest of a hillbilly who'd blown up his fifteen year old "girl wife" with dynamite out at Coffin Rock. What had promised to be a lurid trial, with voyeuristic glimpses into the life of mountain people, ended abruptly when the hillbilly drank poison in his jail cell. Luckily for the *Times*, a group of prospectors rushed into the town of Kelso, claiming they were attacked by apemen the night before. They'd been so scared by the attack that they'd abandoned hundreds of dollars worth of mining equipment during their race back to civilization.

Before Bigfoot went mainstream in the years following World War II, apeman sightings were associated with mining more than any other occupation. In medieval Germany, the Wild Man was even considered to be the symbol of mining. The German town of Wildemann received its name because of a run-in between prospectors and an apeman in the year 1529. To this day the town has a bronze statue of the apeman holding a club in one hand and an uprooted tree in the other.

In the United States, although fur trappers, loggers, and farmers spent a lot of time in the woods, none of them reported seeing apemen nearly as often as the prospectors.

In 1900, the Sixes mining district of Oregon was terrorized by the "Kangaroo Man"—a Bigfoot-type creature who could jump great heights. The New Jersey "Dover Wild Man" of 1894 was last seen heading for the Dickerson mine. In the 1850s, gold miners on Mount Shasta were reportedly attacked by an apeman who came out of nowhere and smashed all their mining equipment. In Southern California, a prospector in 1893 encountered a wild man and noted to a reporter, "The freak bears evidence of having lived underground and was extremely difficult to approach."

In 1900, an Alaskan prospector was chased up a tree by shaggy ape-creatures. In the Alaskan prospector's own words: "I couldn't call them anything but devils, as they were neither men nor monkeys, yet looked like both. They were entirely sexless, their bodies covered with long coarse hair, except where scabs and running sores replaced it."

In 1924, the same year as Ape Canyon, the Canadian prospector Albert Ostman claimed to be abducted by an apeman while looking for a lost goldmine, even living with the apeman's family for a couple days. Ostman eventually escaped by feeding the biggest ape a can of snuff to make it sick, and slipped out while the ape was busy puking. Although this reportedly happened the same year as Ape Canyon, Ostman would not report his story until 1957. Before Ape Canyon, none of these stories were reported above the *extremely* local level, barely making small-town papers, if they were lucky.

The connection between apemen and mining was even more evident during the Ape Canyon incident of 1924. During the days building up to the attack, the prospector Fred Beck remembered that the whole party could hear a pounding sound coming from deep underground. "Sounds like there's a hollow drum in the earth somewhere and something is hitting it." The drumming noise followed them day and night. Beck had no doubt it was the apemen, "but they had not yet appeared in physical form."

Before Bigfoot appeared in physical form the prospectors saw the footprints: two huge tracks in the middle of a sandbar, pressed four inches deep into the wet sand. They were clearly made by something huge, heavy, and almost human, but without shoes.

The most intriguing thing about the tracks was that there were *only* two of them. There were no tracks in the wet sand leading up to the footprints, and there were no tracks leading away from the footprints.

Whatever made them must have materialized right there, and vanished. "No human being could have made these tracks," one of the prospectors said. "And there's only one way they could be made, something dropped from the sky and went back up."

That July the prospectors had just gotten a good assay on the quality of gold on their claim. Nuggets "big as your fingernails" according to Beck. Another prospector said "God or the Devil" would not chase them from St. Helens.

Despite the gold keeping them on the mountain, they were as scared of what awaited them in the woods as people had been of John Tornow. The prospectors wouldn't even walk a hundred yards from the cabin to get spring water without traveling in pairs, armed with rifles. It was while Fred Beck and another prospector were on their way to get water that they first saw an apeman in the furry flesh.

From the top of the canyon they heard a shrill whistle, which was answered by another whistle coming from the opposite cliff. In Puget Sound Indian folklore the apes always carried wooden whistles, which they used to communicate with each other. The whistling was followed by a violent thumping sound "like something was hitting itself on its chest."

The prospectors looked up and saw a black-furred apeman peering down on them from the top of the canyon. His fur was not shaggy like the creatures in Alaska—it was cropped close to the skin—and his face didn't resemble an ape, but a square-jawed manly-man, though he had large, round, bat-like ears.

The prospectors fired their rifles. The apeman ran behind a fir tree. The prospectors blasted away the bark, but not a scratch of fur or ape-flesh. The ape then ran as fast as it could—"fast and upright" according to Beck—all the way to the cover of the forest, where it vanished into the trees.

That night, the prospectors went back to their log cabin, smoked their pipes, ate beans, hotcakes, and settled into a relatively normal evening. Sleeping two to a bunk, head to foot, they went to sleep.

Then the pounding came. Rocks were being thrown against the side of the cabin.

Some Bigfoot books claim the apes were throwing rocks the size of boulders and managed to cave in the roof, but according to Beck this wasn't true, the rocks were much smaller, about the size of baseballs. The roof held up fine, even when apemen started jumping around on it. Reportedly some rocks did fall down the chimney.

A hairy arm reached in through the window and attempted to grab an ax. Beck fired at it and the arm lurched back into the darkness.

Finally, with the sun rising, Beck was able to shoot one of the apes off the edge of a cliff. The ape dropped four hundred feet to the canyon floor. The other apes scattered. Checking where the ape landed, the prospectors could find no trace of a body.

Decades later Beck wrote that after a lifetime of personal experience and research he believed the Bigfoots were creatures from another dimension and were made of spirit-substance which evaporated like water at the moment of death. He claimed, "no one will ever capture one, and no one will ever kill one." Intriguingly, in the Lushootseed language of the Puget Sound Indians, the word for Sasquatch is "Siatko." The "o" sound at the end of "Siatko" connotes something like water or fluidity, an indication that at some point the Indians might have also believed Bigfoot was made of vapor. Later in Fred Beck's life, he claimed to have met a group of Yakama who told him the Siatko used to travel around by floating on their backs downriver like logs, which might also explain the association with water.

The prospectors decided no gold could ever be worth the hassle of inter-dimensional Gorilla Men. That morning they decided to flee their claim, taking only essentials and leaving behind their mining equipment and some sizable nuggets.

On arriving in the town of Kelso, they informed a ranger of their adventures and word spread to *The Seattle Times* correspondent who was in desperate need of a new hillbilly story. Naturally, with the restrictions of a newspaper column, the reporter couldn't include *all* of Fred Beck's story. The full story Beck told is quite a bit weirder than the version printed above.

In the interest of brevity and keeping this book relatively accessible, I decided to cut out the inter-dimensional Indian guide with a magic arrow who led them to the mine in the first place, the magic door to another world which would neither lock nor open, Beck's astral projection to the White House, his encounter with a female ghost/mountain spirit, the lost civilization which once existed in the Cascade Mountains, the magic powers of the volcano, and his faith healing abilities. If you can find a copy, the whole story is available in Beck's book *I Fought the Apemen of Mount St. Helens, WA.* Pieces of the book are excerpted elsewhere, but even the most hippyish, new age, fringy, flying saucer, nutball books about Bigfoot have never dared to print Beck's story in full.

For the 1924 *Seattle Times* article, the spiritual nature of Bigfoot was compressed and greatly secularized. It was reported that they'd been attacked by a previously undiscovered species of ape, with all the inter-dimensional gibberish cut out. This made Bigfoot more accessible to the rationally-minded.

And was it ever accessible. During "the Great Ape Hunt of '24" even a Naval Commander stationed at Bremerton and a local reverend headed out to Mount St. Helens to try and kill the apemen. They were soon joined by a film crew.

Although whites had been seeing ape-like creatures all over the Northwest since at least the 1890s, none of the sightings had ever been treated seriously by a major paper, or ever heard of outside of flannel-land.

During the "Kangaroo Man" scare of 1901, the *Statesman Journal* mocked the reports from prospectors saying, "He is supposed to eat miners raw without any salt, and has been seen to jump from one mountain peak to another, all the while emitting bloodcurdling yells and spouting sulfurous flames from his nostrils. What kind of whiskey do they sell over in that country anyway?" When a wild man was spotted in California in 1904 *The San Bernardino County Sun* similarly joked that "The government ought to get an excise tax on some of the hard cider those people are making."

Why was what would have earlier been dismissed as a crazy hillbilly story now front-page news from Seattle to Portland?

To understand the reason this captured the Seattle imagination, we have to look at some lesser-known local news stories from July of 1924.

Days before the apemen, the *Seattle Times* was running hard-hitting front-page scoops like:

CHARMED LAND

WEATHER IDEAL

BABIES HEALTHY

That was an actual *front-page* headline from July of 1924. The sub-heading elaborated: *Tornadoes Unknown, Roses Bloom at New Year's and Summer Temperatures Are Mild in the Queen City.* In more substantive news, Washington state boasted a $50,000,000 apple crop. It was a wealthy but boring summer, similar to the conditions which would lead to the Bigfoot ape-splosion of the 1950s.

On the national level things were no more eventful. Washington state, along with the rest of the country, had resoundingly elected president Warren G. Harding in 1920 with his promise of a "Return to Normalcy." When Harding died in 1923, his Vice President, Calvin Coolidge, woke up, was sworn into office by his own father, and then went back to sleep. The next morning, he continued to follow through on his predecessor's "Normalcy."

Although in 1919 all of America feared that Seattle's General Strike would lead to a Bolshevik revolution, five years later the fear of anything changing in any substantial way had passed. A few months before the apes were seen in 1924, the Seattle Central Labor Council voted 78 to 71 to purge all Communists from the organization.

The new strategy for organized labor was not to fight management, but to work alongside management with "the union label." Products that were union made carried a special label on them, which all union members were encouraged to buy. The 1919 shout of "They Did It In Russia!" morphed into 1924's "Where Does Your Wife Spend Your Money, Mr. Union Man?" They'd gone from revolution to brand name in five years.

Materially, average people were richer than they had ever been in their lives. One of the reasons so many headed off to fight apemen in 1924 was because it was the first time so many could afford to do so.

The "Gorilla Men" of Ape Canyon were appealing because they provided a primal, wild, way out of a dull, consumeristic, conflict-free life in Seattle.

Naturally, nobody at the time articulated this directly. Before heading to Mount St. Helens with ape-mania, Commander Milo F. Draeml of the United States Navy never said, "I'm going out to the volcano to fight ape-men because modernity is existentially unfulfilling and I no longer have anything bigger than myself to be part of."

Nothing like that was ever said out loud. But from looking at what people wanted out of "Wild Men" before 1924, and what they wanted out of "Wild Men" after 1924, we can get an idea of what was going on.

Before Ape Canyon, even the most outlandish Wild Man stories were usually believed to be white men who had turned feral, like John Tornow, and could be reintegrated into society. Even the Kangaroo Man of 1904 was believed to be "an insane prospector of gigantic stature," according to the *Daily Capital Journal*. A monster terrorizing Granite Falls in 1907, which was referred to by *The Oregon Daily Journal* as "More Beast Than Human," was still believed to be "a Frenchman who took up a timber claim near Mount Pilchuck five years ago and disappeared mysteriously two years later." All of these sightings held up the theory of the frontier that anything wild could be tamed and made white.

Ape Canyon marked a turning point in white consciousness. Having gone as far north and as far west as an American could, the desire was not for a wild that could be tamed, but a wild that was innately wild. You could shave the St. Helens ape, put him in a top hat and monocle, but no matter what, he could never be anything other than a wild, pec-pounding ape.

For days professional hunters, the rising middle class, and scouts for a film crew shot up every inch of St. Helens looking to bag an apeman. Even with the park rangers saying they didn't think they existed, and the locals telling them that Fred Beck was a faith healer kook who believed there were ghosts in his kitchen, they kept searching.

Even after St. Helens erupted in 1980, killing what apes there might have been, people continued to look. They still look now, and to this day the canyon is still Ape Canyon and the nearby lava tube is still the Ape Cave.

To understand why an innately wild, human-but-not-human creature is so popular, particularly to American whites living in the Northwest, requires some cross-cultural perspective.

KINGS AND APES

*T*he Klallam writer Jorg Totsgi was also stunned that whites had seen apemen on Mount St. Helens, but he was more stunned that whites could finally see them. Totsgi was a regular contributor to *The Real American*, an early twentieth century magazine written entirely by and for American Indians. Now it's best remembered for a piece about Native beliefs that he wrote during the Great Ape Hunt of '24 that ran in various Northwest newspapers. According to Totsgi, all Indians knew that the creatures existed, but no Indian had seen one since 1909 and it was generally believed they'd gone extinct.

Many old Puget Sound Indians never understood the white fascination with Bigfoot, particularly because until Bigfoot made the papers they had no idea there was anything unusual about them.

Before the arrival of the whites, the Duwamish River was infested with apes every year during the salmon run. They could easily be seen swatting salmon out of the river like bears with their hairy ape paws, and they frequently stole fish from the fishermen's nets. Suquamish elders living into the 1940s recalled that there used to be so many apes along the river that a member of Chief Seattle's tribe once chucked a deer bone into some bushes and inadvertently hit an ape on the head. The writer Ernest Bertelson met many Suquamish elders who told him stories about people they knew who'd gotten the crap beaten out of them by apes.

According to the elders interviewed by Bertelson, the apes were so strong that they "scorned to use weapons." Normally they just snapped necks, killing their victims instantly. One Suquamish man bumped into an ape who slammed him into a hazel bush so hard that it broke both his legs. The ape then grabbed a vine and tied the man to a tree branch by his testicles. The Suquamish man's friends found him dangling there.

When anthropologist Wayne Suttles was showing a book of animals to the Lummi elder Julius Charles, the elder mentioned an animal was missing from the book. "It was like a man but shaggy like a bear, like a big monkey 7 feet tall. They went away when the Whites came. The Indians never killed any; it was a pretty wise animal, or whatever you call it."

Jorg Totsgi, writing in 1924, said that his own Klallam tribe and the apemen spoke the same language, as they were both descended from bears. In the 1890s a Klallam man named Henry Napoleon had visited the Bigfoot homeland while on a trip to see family on Vancouver Island. According to Napoleon, the Bigfoots lived in a large cave hidden in the center of the island. He claimed to know this because they supposedly took him down there to show him around.

While in the cave the apes showed Napoleon the secret ointment that they used to turn invisible. It was believed that during the distant past the apemen and humans had been relatively similar, the difference being that the apemen lacked the ability to take on human souls. Anyone familiar with the Native religions of Puget Sound will be aware that the word "soul" can mean about fifty thousand different things in their original languages. Which kind of "soul" Totsgi had in mind is now lost, but the humans became human, and the apes remained as they'd always been.

Culturally, the most important detail in Henry Napoleon's story is that a Klallam man placed the homeland of the apemen on Vancouver Island, home of the wealthier and more hierarchical Kwakiutl and Nootka cultures. Whereas, among the less hierarchical Puget Sound tribes, the apemen play an extremely minor role in their belief system (basically regarded as an urban legend or nuisance), in the wealthier northern cultures of the Haida, Kwakiutl, Tsimshian, and Nootka, the concept of the Wild Man was traditionally a central part of their worldview.

Anthropologically, the cultures of Haida Gwaii and Vancouver Island more resembled semi-feudal agricultural societies than they did the hunter-gatherer cultures found to the south. Due to the enormous wealth of the Pacific Ocean, the coastal people could harvest fields of shellfish twice a day and could hunt herds of seals and sea lions. As the Haida translator Robert Bringhurst phrased it, "the Haida planted no crops, and yet they lived, like wealthy farmers, in substantial towns."

With their wealth, the Haida had a more stratified society compared to Suquamish or Duwamish peoples. The Haida term for "aristocrat" literally means "real person" or "genuine person," implying that non-aristocrats are actually less real.

Like 19th century whites, Haida traditionally believed that a man who became lost in the woods could physically transform, turning hairy and feral. One of the Haida words for Wild Man, *Gagiit*, translates to "man on all fours." Unlike the whites, however, the Haida did not believe that a *Gagiit* could be transformed back into a human.

Robert Cogo, a 2oth century Haida historian and storyteller, remembered hearing a story of the *Gagiit* as told by his father, Eddie, who was born in 1860 and raised in the final decades of the traditional Haida culture. According to Eddie Cogo, a hunting party once encountered a *Gagiit*. "The figure was hard to look at. What once was a human being was now a weird-looking wild man." It was trying to warm itself on a rock when the Haida hunters "decided to put the *Gagiit* out of its misery." The best shot in the group killed the abomination that violated the separation between man and wild. According to Eddie Cogo, "The creature was buried on the edge of the beach and to this day this place is tabu to Haidas."

Despite being covered in fur, *Gagiit* are always depicted as cold, possibly a commentary on the hostility of the non-human world. When writing of another man who was in the process of turning *Gagiit*, Robert Cogo wrote, "They tried to warm him before the fire, the change was too great. He died. This is the end of my story."

In some Haida myths, contact with the Wild Men was conversely considered to be an auspicious encounter. One Wild Man myth in particular is uncanny in its similarity to those found in hierarchical agricultural societies all over the world from medieval Europe to ancient Mesopotamia. It gives crucial insight into understanding why apemen were so popular with white America in the years after WWII.

In the myth, a Chief's nephew is so lazy and coddled that he is in danger of losing his aristocratic status (in classical Haida culture the maternal uncle's relationship to his favorite nephew is the most sacred family relationship and the one that determines inheritance). One night the youth is visited by a Wild Man in bearskin who helps him train so that he is strong enough to reign. As soon as the Wild Man helps the future chief maintain his position of power, he disappears back into the wilderness.

This is widely considered to be one of the oldest stories in the world, as a Wild Man helping a king maintain his power can also be found in the 3,000+ year old Mesopotamian *Epic of Gilgamesh*.

In the story, rather than being too weak, King Gilgamesh is so powerful that he has lost touch with his humanity. His subjects pray to the gods for something to give King Gilgamesh self-control and the gods respond by making a kind of gollum Wild Man out of clay to wrestle the mighty Gilgamesh.

Although Gilgamesh wins the wrestling match, the Wild Man, Enkidu, becomes his closest friend and helps him to become a more just ruler. Together they team up to tear down the cedar forests, indicating the belief that the desire to get in touch with the wild is not actually a desire to live harmoniously with it. Unlike most cultures, the ancient Mesopotamians were apparently aware that the kind of "Wild" represented by the Wild Man Enkidu was an artificial wild meant to serve civilization.

In the cedar forest Gilgamesh and Enkidu meet the ugly, poison-breathed guardian spirit Humbaba. Being the real representative of the natural world, Humbaba can instantly tell that Enkidu is an artificial creature. Whereas the rest of Mesopotamia is fooled by the shaggy hair that covers Enkidu's whole body, Humbaba knows that beneath the fur, Enkidu is made of clay and is more robot than ape. To highlight Enkidu's unnaturalness Humbaba angrily calls him a thing "who sucked no mother's milk!" Gilgamesh and his faux-ape companion then ruthlessly destroy Humbaba's forest.

Enkidu is a tool meant to help Gilgamesh (who represents civilization) and once he has fulfilled his purpose, the gods kill him off. In most cultures, at some point the Wild Man needs to die no matter how much he is honored. The story of the death of a Wild Man plays a crucial role in the mythology of the Kwakiutl tribe of Vancouver Island. Their variation on the Wild Man has many names, mainly known as the Man Eater. Of all the secret societies the Kwakiutl have, historically the Man Eater Society—the *hamatsa*—was the most exclusive, only for the elite.

Young men being prepared for positions of leadership would be picked by the society and sent out in the woods to get in touch with the "wild." The great Jewish-German anthropologist Franz Boas—who studied the Kwakiutl in the 1880s—referred to these young men as "initiates," although this is a poor translation. Boas's partner—the half-white, half-Tlingit artist and writer George Hunt—more accurately translated "initiate" as "go through the rules."

The most famous picture of a Kwakiutl man going through the *hamatsa* process does look wild—that's the whole point—he is shirtless with ferns wrapped around his wrists and head. His lips whistle as Wild Men's lips do in masks and his eyes roll up towards heaven like his body has been possessed by the spirit of a monster.

However, a closer look at the photo shows that the ferns he wears on his head have been twisted into symbolic shapes not found in nature, and he is wearing pants. Although it seems he is embracing the wild, George Hunt realized he is actually following a rigid set of rules. Rules ultimately designed to help him maintain power over others.

Another Kwakiutl name for the Wild Man revealingly translates as "Wishing To Be Tamed."

According to multiple Kwakiutl accounts—collected from different communities all over Vancouver Island—the *hamatsa* society and their ritual began in the ancient past when some Kwakiutl brothers got lost on a hunting trip. They came across a quiet house out in the woods where blood red smoke rose from the chimney.

Cautiously, they entered the house and at first thought it empty, but then noticed a woman whose legs had turned to roots, which anchored her to the dirt floor.

She told them she was the wife of the shaggy "Man Eater." He so dominated her that he'd attached her to the floor, this way she'd never be able to leave the house. The brothers offered to rescue her but instead she asked that they hide and kill the Man Eater.

"I went all around the world to find food!" sang the Man Eater on coming home.

"I went all around the world to find human flesh!"

"I went all around the world to find human heads!"

"I went all around the world to find corpses!"

The thing the Kwakiutl heroes saw enter the house was barely even a Wild Man. He had become so powerful that his shaggy body had grown starving, hungry mouths all over it. He was so powerful that nothing could control him, not even himself. Driven entirely by appetites that could never be satisfied or stopped, he'd become full-master and full-slave in one body.

Franz Boas translated "Man Eater" as "Cannibal," but as George Hunt pointed out, this is a bad translation. The Man Eater can not be a cannibal because he has lost the ability to recognize humans as his own kind. To the Man Eater, everything that is not him is only food.

Although named "Wishing To Be Tamed" the brothers realized that nothing can be done to save this creature, except kill it.

After the brothers killed the Man Eater, they once again tried to rescue his wife. Her roots were so firmly attached to the dirt floor that severing them would kill her. Instead, she asked that they leave her there to die and go back to their people so they can learn from the Man Eater through the *hamatsa*.

In addition to being the name of the society, the word *hamatsa* also refers to the dance performed by society members at the Winter Ceremonials.

In the ceremony, the man possessed by the spirit of the Man Eater ferociously dances while the other dancers attempt to tame him. Attempts are made to control him through song, but the only thing that can get the Man Eater to behave is human flesh.

Whether or not actual human flesh was used historically has never been revealed, but the current *hamatsa* ceremony no longer uses it (if they ever did).

It is intentionally unclear how real anything in the ceremony actually is. The word for performing a religious ceremony—*tsetesqua*—is the same word that can be used to accuse somebody of cheating at gambling. Boas translated it as "fraudulent, pretended, to cheat" and was extremely confused by this. In his writings he wondered if the Kwakiutl thought their religion was fake.

There are probably multiple reasons for how this word choice came around. The Kwakiutl were historically a warrior culture, and for men trained to be leading other warriors in combat (the *hamatsa* was only for the elite) it was important to be suspicious of everything seen and heard, hence even a skeptical attitude towards the most sacred customs.

Another possible reason they used the word "fraud" was because, like the ancient Mesopotamians who wrote Gilgamesh, they were aware that Man Eater does not represent the real "wild," but only a fake wild used for control.

Even at his wildest, the dancer taking on the role of the Man Eater dances to an extremely complicated syncopated rhythm. One of the main things that separates humans from apes is that apes have no sense of rhythm. Chimpanzees cannot be taught to follow a metronome. While the Man Eater appears out of control and in need of taming, the dancer shows off that he has artfully mastered the choreography and is fully prepared to be chief of the village when his time comes.

Whether in a Potlatch house on Vancouver Island, a castle in Medieval France, or on the shores of ancient Mesopotamia, under the skin of an apeman there is a king. This connection between Wild Men and kings can be found all over medieval Europe. King Charles VI of France once inadvertently lit himself on fire while dressed like a Wild Man at a masquerade ball. The same basic story as Enkidu and Gilgamesh is a common European folktale, most famously known as the Brothers Grimm story, "Iron Hans." In the German version, a young prince is playing with his ball when it accidently rolls into the cage of a Wild Man who is kept in the courtyard. The Wild Man makes a deal with the boy, saying that he will only give the ball back if the prince opens the cage and releases him. As soon as the Wild Man is released, he grabs the prince and carries him off into the woods. Through a rigorous fitness regime, he trains the prince to be worthy of marrying the beautiful princess.

If "Iron John" sounds familiar, you may recall the book *Iron John: A Book About Men* that came out in 1990. It started a goofy New Age men's movement where middle-aged, middle-class, suburban white men went off into the woods to try and get in touch with their wild masculine nature.

"Iron John" might also sound familiar because it is the same basic trope behind the "Magic Negro" stereotype, a term coined by Spike Lee. This character is presented in movies such as *The Legend of Bagger Vance* or *The Green Mile*. From Gilgamesh to *The Green Mile,* a character in a position of authority needs the help of someone or something from a perceived lower standing to give them "earthier," less cerebral wisdom. This can also be seen when looking back at the story of Gilgamesh. According to Harvard professor Dr. William Moran, the character of Enkidu was largely based on anti-primitivism writings, in which the world's first city dwellers compared hunter-gatherers to animals, thus placing Enkidu as a monster rather than a sidekick. It was not until their hierarchical, urban culture started to suffocate the inhabitants of the Middle East's great walled kingdoms that they looked to these classist stereotypes for an antidote to tyrannous kings.

The contradiction here is that the role of the Wild Man does not exist to overthrow these kings or despots, but rather he exists to help them maintain power. The Wild Man is a tool, and from Gilgamesh to *The Green Mile*, once they have served their function they either disappear or die.

ROUSSEAU AND DAHINDEN

*T*he similarities between Jean-Jacques Rousseau (popularizer of the "Noble Savage" cliche) and René Dahinden (obsessive Bigfoot hunter) are absolutely uncanny.

Both were Swiss, and despite Rousseau being born in 1704 and René Dahinden being born in 1930, both were the products of abusive Swiss upbringings. Abandoned by their families at young ages, Rousseau was apprenticed to an engraver who regularly beat him, and Dahinden was effectively enslaved by a Swiss farmer who treated him "five steps lower than a dog" according to Dahinden's book on Bigfoot.

Both Rousseau and Dahinden turned to the wide open spaces for relief from the screwed-up world of people. Famously enjoying long walks in the country, a young Rousseau was once out so long that when he returned to his walled city the gate had been locked until the next morning. After spending the night sleeping outside the wall he reported late for his apprenticeship and the master engraver beat Rousseau so savagely that, at the age of fifteen, he ran away from home forever.

Similarly, at fifteen René Dahinden also ran away from life on the farm. Years later Dahinden jokingly sent a thank you letter to his former foster father/landlord, saying after living under him any hardship he experienced in the outside world "was a joke."

Despite both of them being Swiss, they are usually mistaken for being from the countries that they later fled to; Rousseau incorrectly being classified as a "French" philosopher and Dahinden mistakenly being classified as a "French-Canadian"

Bigfoot hunter. If you've ever seen the Bigfoot movie *Harry and the Hendersons* the French-Canadian villain out to kill Bigfoot is based on Dahinden.

One evening, after finishing his work on a farm in the Canadian province of Alberta, Dahinden listened to a CBC radio report about an expedition to hunt the Yeti in the Himalayas. Dahinden turned to his boss. "Wouldn't that be something, to be on the hunt for that thing?"

"Hell," his boss replied. "You don't have to go that far; they got them things in British Columbia."

That one casual comment in 1953 completely changed Dahinden's life. It was like "A switch suddenly turning on in my head," Dahinden later wrote. "It seemed like a great adventure."

The adventure would last for the next forty-eight years, until his death in 2001.

Jean-Jacques Rousseau, however, could never have gone off into the wilderness to search for the Wild Man on account of a painful bladder problem. It required him to wear baggy Armenian pants to hide his catheter and, of course, an Armenian fur hat and coat to match the pants.

Instead Rousseau searched for the Wild Man from the comfort of Paris, trying to figure out what people were originally like before they were destroyed by civilization. The term "Noble Savage"—or "Bon Sauvage" in French—does not appear anywhere in Rousseau's writing, but he does write about "sauvages" frequently and he forever popularized the stereotype.

To be fair to Rousseau, at the time of his writing, "savage" did not necessarily have any negative connotations. It meant "wild" in the spirit of a majestic horse or a free flying eagle. In western Europe "Savage" is even a common last name, along with its Germanic variations of "Wild, Wilde, Dewilde, Vilde, Wyeld, Wield, and Whilde."

After running away from the engraver, Rousseau faced constant disappointment and betrayal from every level of society, ranging from ambassadors to philosophers, to the lower classes and even to himself. He came to the conclusion that the problem was his entire culture. To him, writing the story of western civilization "shall be telling that of human sickness." He contrasted the sickness of Europeans with the "good constitutions of the savages."

Like most writers who attack "civilization," he was hit by the problem of what to compare it to. There has been a bad habit in anthropology from before even Rousseau's time until now to treat hunter-gatherer peoples like "natural" people. City people can be compared to them in the same way a pigeon raised in captivity can be compared to a wild bird.

With humans, no such comparison can be made. Different hunter-gatherer societies have distinct cultures that vary too greatly from each other to ever speak of a generic "hunter-gatherer philosophy." Still, from Rousseau's time until now we have been saddled with the generic textbook idea of an "indigenous person" in order to make it possible to contrast and trash city folk.

The "savages" that Rousseau writes about are based on European mythological ideas of "Wild Men" more than they are on any actual peoples. He did not believe hunter-gatherers to be fully human, writing that "there is still a greater difference between savage and civilized man, than between wild and tame beasts."

Rousseau even believed that the native peoples of Africa and America were so close to wild animals that other animals could recognize that quality in them and not see them as a threat. "This is doubtless why negroes and savages are so little afraid of the wild beasts they may meet in the woods." It was a quality he regrettably believed Europeans had lost, their "effeminate way of life" sucking their strength and leading them into "deeper degeneracy."

He eventually became one of the first of many thinkers to lump children, animals, and hunter-gatherer peoples all into the same category. All three of these things are somehow supposed to provide a window into a world of lost purity. However, in his more lucid moments, Rousseau realized that his idealized view of nature and natural man "perhaps never existed, and probably never will." Despite this, his philosophies and writings remain some of the most influential in history, and every single person reading this has been either directly or indirectly influenced by his beliefs on nature and humanity.

Towards the end of René Dahinden's life, he had alienated everybody he'd ever known by his uncompromising search for the Wild Man. And, like Rousseau, he was becoming skeptical of their existence. "You know," he told one of his few remaining friends. "I've spent over 40 years—and I didn't find it. I guess that's got to say something."

Living out of two trailers in the Vancouver wilderness, he never gave up the search. While he never found the Wild Man, his disgust with all aspects of civilization grew. A reporter who visited him shortly before his death noted the way Dahinden closely glared at him without saying a word while smoking on his pipe by the campfire. Eventually Dahinden spoke only to voice his complaints about all the con-artists selling fake prints, the crackpots, and those only after Bigfoot for the glory.

Despite his disdain for people just after Bigfoot for the money, Dahinden himself had commercialized Bigfoot by appearing in a Kokanee beer commercial in which Bigfoot steals all the beer out of his trailer while Dahinden's back is turned. It was the closest Dahinden ever came to finding Bigfoot.

"It's getting to the point where if I saw a Bigfoot in the flesh, I think I'd leave it alone and not tell anybody," he told the reporter. He said he couldn't stand to see people try to get a slice of glory out of it.

He was apparently so anti-social that he could not even stand being around other anti-social Bigfoot hunters. As different as Rousseau and Dahinden's approaches were to trying to find the "Wild Man," both were motivated out of an intense dislike of modern people and the need to find an alternative.

When Rousseau died in 1778, no European had ever even seen Puget Sound, let alone all of the Americas. To him the world was still a massive unexplored place filled with what he thought were wild, free, child-like people.

Dahinden began his search for Bigfoot in 1953, the same year that Mount Everest was first summited. Nowhere was left unexplored, no people were left alone. It is no coincidence that after the Pacific Northwest, the area most commonly associated with apemen is the Himalayas. Both were places that the two would have seen as mysterious, and possibly even unconquerable.

CRIPPLE FOOT

D r. Grover Krantz—professor of physical anthropology at Washington State University—was excited to learn of the "Cripple Foot" tracks found in the snow in the tiny mining town of Bossburg, Washington in the winter of 1969. According to the footprints, this Bigfoot had one shriveled, deformed foot, meaning it would be easier to catch.

Taking a break from his lectures, Dr. Krantz headed up to Bossburg to investigate for himself. Today Bossburg is a ghost town, and even back in 1969 it was dying. In the ongoing connection between Bigfoot and mining, new mines apparently produced robust Bigfoots like the kind that threw rocks at Fred Beck, whereas the exhausted lead and silver mines of Bossburg produced a disabled Bigfoot. The locals believed Bigfoot was digging through their garbage for food, as he could no longer survive in the wild.

Dr. Krantz knew from personal experience what good luck a broken foot could bring. As a 6 foot, 3 inch giant with enormous hands and an enormous intellect, he did not have any self-control while a student at Berkeley. Argumentative and opinionated, he'd already been married and divorced twice while still a grad student and had to drop out of his doctoral program after getting into a fight with a professor. Dr. Krantz wrote that "My life at that time consisted of a part-time job and nearly full-time drinking."

While working his part-time job at the Berkeley museum, Dr. Krantz dropped the Dead Sea Scrolls on his foot, crushing his big toe, requiring him to cut back on his famous 24-hour to 36-hour hard drinking parties in the 1960s.

Unable to work until his foot healed, he was fortunate enough to meet Evelyn Einstein, a ballerina who claimed to be the illegitimate daughter of Albert Einstein. She took Dr. Krantz in while he recuperated and became his third out of four wives. With her support and that of an Irish Wolfhound puppy, he was able to control his self-destructive behavior long enough to get his doctorate.

He would soon learn that publicly searching for an unknown ape is more damaging to an academic career than being a temperamental drunk ever was.

When Dr. Krantz was making casts at Bossburg, Bigfoots seemed more common than squirrels. Since the end of World War II, their footprints had been showing up everywhere from British Columbia to Northern California. Whereas before the war most Northwesterns had never even heard of "Bigfoot" or "Sasquatch," by the 1960s there were few people in all of North America who didn't know that apemen supposedly lived in the Northwest forests.

From 1959 to 1962, a ridiculously rich Texas oilman named Tom Slick financed a massive expedition to search for Bigfoot, employing dozens of trackers and hunters. To Dr. Krantz's great annoyance, Tom Slick never shared any of his research. The research remained secret even after Slick died in a plane crash while returning from a Canadian hunting trip in 1962.

Not that Dr. Krantz needed Tom Slick. Bigfoots were now so plentiful that even the police were seeing them. The summer before the Bossburg "Cripple Foot" tracks, a deputy sheriff in Grays Harbor, Washington had to slam on the brakes one night while driving to the beach because a Bigfoot was blocking the road. At first deputy sheriff Verlin Herrington thought the thing in his headlights was a bear standing on its hind legs. Then he noticed that unlike a bear it had no snout, and instead of paws it had fingers and toes.

He considered shooting it in the leg with his revolver in order to follow the blood trail the next morning in the daylight, but decided against it. In the nineteenth century the Nisqually war leader Chief Leschi allegedly once shot a Sasquatch and followed its blood trail, but then lost sight of it. History has shown that you can shoot a Sasquatch and still lose sight of it. Deputy Herrington chose to let it go. A major mistake.

Deputy Herrington had no intention of telling the media, but after he was overheard at a cafe talking about it with his fellow officers, it became a major news story. A photograph of an enormous footprint was taken near where he claimed to have seen the ape, but it was not enough to save his reputation. Deputy Verrington was dropped from the police force. No reason was given as to why, but it was speculated that it was because a deputy who claimed to see Bigfoot could not be used as a credible witness in other cases.

At first Dr. Krantz was equally apprehensive about publicly admitting he believed in Bigfoot. The footprints found at Bossburg looked real, but when a reporter asked Dr. Krantz if he thought Bigfoot actually existed, Dr. Krantz would only reply "the evidence was very impressive." He sent the evidence off to top experts in various kinds of fields all over the world before he would publicly state his opinion.

A Bigfoot hunter has to be vigilant because in the world of apeman research there are not only fake Bigfoots, but fake fake-Bigfoots. For a variety of reasons there are almost as many people who have lied about faking Bigfoot as there are people who have lied about having seen Bigfoot.

Numerous people have claimed that they "invented" Bigfoot as a hoax, most famously Ray Wallace in California. This, however, seems more than unlikely as stories of Wild Men have been found in a myriad of cultures all over the world for thousands of years. No one person could have ever "created" Bigfoot. Yet *The Seattle Times* gullibly published the headline in 2002 "Loveable Trickster Created a Monster with Bigfoot Hoax," and uncritically published Ray Wallace's family's claims that he created Bigfoot by tying boards to his feet and walking around in the woods.

Some people seek attention by claiming they saw a monster, and some people seek attention by claiming they made up a monster.

While the Bossburg "Cripple Foot" tracks looked good to Dr. Krantz, to be sure they weren't created by some "prankster," he sent them off to the University of Groningen in the Netherlands for analysis. Professor A.G. de Wilde examined them and concluded that the prints had to have come from a living animal, as the toes could clearly still move. The casts were then sent to the FBI and Scotland Yard. John Berry, the world's top forensic fingerprint analyst at the time—or, technically, "dermal ridge" analyst—and editor of *Fingerprint Whorld* also confirmed that the prints were real.

Dr. Krantz named his new discovery *Gigantopithecus canadensis*, but was surprised when the scientific discovery of the century went unnoticed. "I was just as naive as any of the younger scientists today, perhaps more," Dr. Krantz wrote about his attempts to find a publisher. "The idea that such studies ought *not* to be published never occurred to me." After nine scholarly journals rejected his findings, they were eventually published in *Northwest Anthropological Research Notes*. The findings were again ignored.

Or ignored by most people. Washington State University, where he taught anthropology, took note. "My first shock was to be deferred on tenure for one year, in spite of the fact that I was already more frequently cited for my normal work than most of the other members of the department." At first he thought the controversy would blow over after a couple years, but then his promotion to full professor was denied. When he asked for explanation, "the only reason the dean could come up with was that my work was not favorably received in all quarters. (By this criterion, Charles Darwin and Albert Einstein could not possibly have gotten this promotion at my university.)"

To back up his research he had hair samples, footprints, footage, and eyewitness testimony. "The legal profession regularly convicts and kills people on a tiny fraction of the kind of evidence that we already have for the sasquatch," Krantz angrily wrote.

Although he thought he had more than enough hard evidence, he took comfort in the fact that when the paleoanthropologist Eugene Dubois first found the "missing link" Java Man fossil in the 1890s, nobody in Europe would acknowledge them for decades, and when Raymond Dart discovered the first "missing link" *Australopithecus* fossil in the 1920s, nobody would recognize that either.

Scientifically, the existence of Bigfoot is not that far-fetched. Apes do exist in Asia and Africa. It was not like Dr. Krantz was out searching for dragons or chupacabras. There are plenty of creatures known to science that make Sasquatch seem as normal as a raccoon. There are thousands of deep sea creatures and microscopic organisms that look like monsters out of a sci-fi movie. All of these creatures have been documented and observed and are undeniably much stranger than Bigfoot. If you were to put pictures of anything found under a microscope or from the depths of the ocean in a cheesy cryptozoology book, most people would think they were inventions as well.

For some reason, Dr. Krantz found people with no background in biology and anthropology were deeply emotionally invested in disproving Bigfoot. Throughout his career he frequently puzzled over why they cared this much, since they never cared about his work on Indo-European languages, coyote bones, or *Homo erectus* and *Ramapithecus* fossils. "When asked for their thoughts on a subject where they have little or no information, most people will not express any firm opinion," Dr. Krantz wrote. "The average person does not know whether a steam engine is more or less efficient than an internal combustion engine and will usually say so; most biologists are equally ignorant of this subject and will also freely admit it. But if you ask these same people whether Bigfoot exists, a subject on which they are in most cases equally uninformed, a surprising number will state definitely 'yes' or 'no.' There must be some good reason for this irrational behavior; there appears to be something in this subject that strikes deep emotional roots."

While to Dr. Krantz Bigfoot was just an undiscovered species of animal, he noted that to most, Bigfoot represented a "missing link" between man and nature.

Some did not want this link, as according to Dr. Krantz, "They find it emotionally satisfying to believe that there is a vast, unoccupied gulf separating us from the rest of the animal kingdom."

He is not particularly talking about creationists or people opposed to evolution. While now the Northwest has an eco-friendly image, that was not always the case. The old Northwesterners of the World War II generation truly believed the entire universe ended at their property lines. They didn't want a "missing link" connecting them to the natural world any more than they wanted a link connecting them to their neighbors. Anybody who thinks Seattle culture is closed off *now* should have met my grandfather.

In 1958 the King County Taxpayer's League formed to block the construction of a sewage treatment plant, believing they could dump untreated human and industrial waste into Lake Washington without consequences. The head of the league, a Renton lawyer named Nicholas A. Maffeo, wrote, "I wish to say, my friends, in all earnestness that if it came to a choice between 'loss' of Lake Washington or loss of any part of our American heritage of freedom, I would personally choose to lose Lake

Washington." He even proposed draining the Lake and filling it in. Dr. Edmondson, head of the organization in charge of cleaning the Lake, was aware of "the man from Renton" and wrote that, if you were familiar with Washington State politics, his ideas "made a weird sort of sense."

The connection between anti-environmentalism and not wanting to believe there is a link between the human and natural world led Dr. Krantz to suspect that the Northwest lumber industry might be involved in covering up Bigfoot's existence. "Considering the recent fuss over the snail darter, a tiny fish that delayed dam building for years, and the current strife over the northern spotted owl, the discovery of an animal like the sasquatch would have a devastating impact," Krantz wrote.

As he came into contact with more and more cranks claiming to be in psychic contact with Bigfoot (with the elusive cryptid communicating with them telepathically), Dr. Krantz started to believe many of them might actually be employed by the lumber industry to destroy the credibility of serious researchers. "The most effective approach would be for such persons to loudly proclaim the existence of the sasquatch and to offer totally unacceptable evidence to support their contention. In fact, the more absurd the evidence, the more effective it would be to make the whole subject look ridiculous."

Although he wouldn't name names, Dr. Krantz did mention one person who "has had no visible means of support for the last fifteen years that I have known of his antics; if he is not being paid for this, it's rather difficult to explain why he's doing it." Considering some of the incredible crackpots and misfits who have been involved in Bigfoot hunting, there are hundreds of people he could be referring to.

As Dr. Krantz was one of the only legitimate scientists interested in Bigfoot, he was constantly being contacted by all kinds of weirdos. "The lunatic fringe has the sasquatch moving through space-time warps, riding in UFOs, making telepathic connections, showing superior intelligence, and the like." To Dr. Krantz the main thing they all had in common was that "It is tantamount to academic suicide to become associated with any of these people." Having personally met many Bigfoot nuts,

I doubt any of them are actually paid by the lumber industry, as Dr. Krantz speculated.

Like those who hate Bigfoot, many who love him also think of Bigfoot as a link to the natural world. According to Dr. Krantz, "People who lean toward this view seem to eagerly accept the sasquatch as providing us with that link to the rest of the animal kingdom. They find it emotionally satisfying to believe in the existence of a species that seems to constitute this 'missing link.'"

Part of this was an age thing. Those opposed to Bigfoot in the 1970s tended to be older. Dr. Krantz wrote that by the 1980s most of the people at his university who had been most opposed to his research on Bigfoot had all either quit or retired, and the younger generation who replaced them was more open to the idea of an apeman in the Northwest woods.

Bigfoot's biggest fanbase is, was, and always will be composed of white Baby Boomers. They made up the bulk of Dr. Krantz's much loathed "lunatic fringe." I personally found out why while attending the 2019 Sasquatch Summit at the Quinault Beach Resort & Casino.

BIGFOOT CONVENTION

*T*he odd thing about Bigfoot nuts is how normal they are. People into aliens are weird, people into ghosts are weird, people into subterranean monsters known as "deros" are extremely weird; but at the Sasquatch Summit at the Quinault Beach Resort & Casino the audience looked like the same kind of audience that would attend any event geared towards old Baby Boomers who wear a lot of flannel.

A guy who looked like a small town high school gym teacher nearing retirement told me in all seriousness that he once passed out in the woods and Sasquatch carried him back to his porch. "I wish I could choose not to believe in Sasquatch," he told me, "but I was never given that privilege."

"What did Sasquatch smell like?" I asked him.

"Clean. Like a shaggy dog that an owner takes care of. They bath in running rivers. The Sasquatch people take better care of themselves than most people in Seattle."

Among Bigfoot fans, if you refer to Bigfoot as a "Sasquatch *person*" that means you believe Bigfoot is not only an unknown species of ape, but a semi-spiritual creature with superhuman intelligence. Dr. Krantz never even capitalized the word "sasquatch" to highlight his belief that it was a perfectly ordinary animal no different from a raccoon or a panda.

"I wish I could choose not to believe in Sasquatch," is one of the most common expressions at the convention among those who claim to have seen one. Nobody has said it more throughout their life than the old cowboy Bob Gimlin, who was at the convention signing posters. He was the main reason I'd gone all the way from Seattle to the edge of the Olympic Peninsula.

Even if you haven't heard of the Patterson-Gimlin film of 1967, you've seen the footage in any Bigfoot documentary ever. Besides Kennedy getting shot in the head, no other grainy 20 seconds of home video footage from the 1960s has been subject to as much debate, study, and controversy as the footage of a female Sasquatch walking towards the woods, glancing back at the camera and continuing to walk.

Roger Patterson was a sleazy rodeo cowboy from eastern Washington, who before stumbling upon the Bigfoot he filmed in Northern California, had been planning on making a fictional film about the Ape Canyon incident of 1924. To show how little people cared about Bigfoot before the Baby Boomers, Roger Patterson wrote that although he'd spent the first 28 years of his life in Yakima, he had never heard of "the hairy apes of Mt. St. Helens" until he went off to California in the early 1960s, despite St. Helens being "only seventy miles from home as the crow flies."

To prepare for the film, Roger Patterson interviewed Fred Beck and noted that at first the old mountain man was "reluctant to speak much of his experience; I suppose because of all the ridicule he had taken over the years." Patterson was the only person to ever notice this quality in Beck, as every other person who interviewed him noted that you couldn't get him to shut up about all his hillbilly superstitions.

In Patterson's movie, Bob Gimlin was going to play the Indian guide who brought Beck and the other prospectors to the goldmine. It was never clear who was going to play Bigfoot or how they were going to show him.

Naturally, many people believe that the Bigfoot in the footage is the suit that Patterson planned on using for his film. Over four people have come forward claiming to be the one in the suit, but none of them have been able to produce it or provide any proof that they even knew Roger Patterson.

When I got a chance to speak with Bob Gimlin at the Sasquatch Summit, I asked him what Roger Patterson's plans were for filming the fake Bigfoot in his movie. Gimlin told me, "Roger never planned much of anything."

To support Gimlin's claim, after filming the Bigfoot Patterson sold the film rights to numerous, overlapping individuals, not thinking through the legal predicament he got himself into. The overlapping film rights made it difficult to find a good copy of the film for decades. Dr. Krantz, who knew Patterson well, wrote, "In my judgement of his character, Patterson might have tried to fake a film of this kind if he had the ability to do so. Also in my judgement he had nowhere near the knowledge or facilities to do so—nor, for that matter, had anyone else."

When the Disney executive Ken Peterson viewed the film in 1969, he confirmed that even Disney would not be able to duplicate it. Gordon Valient, the head research scientist for Nike, also confirmed that the thing in the footage did not walk like a human, and he specialized in human locomotion.

Many biologists were quick to debunk it, but as Dr. Krantz pointed out, most of these debunkers also bragged that they'd never even seen the footage.

If anyone had a reason to reveal the footage was fake, it was Bob Gimlin. Despite his name being in the title "Patterson-Gimlin Film," Roger Patterson screwed him out of all the royalties. When Dr. Krantz brought Gimlin a cast of a Bigfoot footprint taken from the site of the filming, Gimlin asked if he could keep it since Patterson had never even given him one of the casts. For decades Gimlin would not even publicly comment on the film, wanting to put it behind him.

However, he now signs posters for $20.00 a piece at Bigfoot conventions and has a DVD for sale, so he's not completely disinterested in whether or not that footage is real.

Whether or not Roger Patterson faked the footage, nobody doubts that he believed Bigfoot was real. If he had faked the footage, he would have faked it again instead of wasting the money from it on increasingly bizarre Bigfoot hunts. Shortly before his death, Patterson blew all of his money attempting to rescue a Sasquatch that he heard was being held captive in a Buddhist monastery in Thailand. Not even most of the Bigfoot nuts at the convention I went to would have fallen for that one.

One reason Patterson devoted the last years of his life to hunting for Bigfoot was because he was diagnosed with a terminal case of Hodgkin's Lymphoma. He thought that if he captured Bigfoot he could somehow make enough money to cure himself.

It was a horrible get-rich-quick scheme, but he was still one of the few people in the history of Bigfoot hunting who had a coherent reason to try and find Bigfoot.

Dr. Krantz spent at least $100,000 of his own money looking for Bigfoot, greatly harming his academic career, and by the time of his death in 2002 had nothing to show for it, never even having seen Bigfoot himself. However, he continued to teach after his death, donating his skeleton to George Washington University.

In Dr. Krantz's case, one of his main motivations for looking for Bigfoot was his all consuming desire to prove to the world that the cryptid truly does exist. If the scientific community had merely been indifferent to his research, instead of openly hostile towards it, he probably never would have taken it as far as he did. He was also a generation older than the typical Bigfoot fan, being born in 1931 instead of 1951, so he is not a normal example of Bigfoot fandom.

Bigfoot became a phenomena because of the Baby Boomers. According to the *Bigfoot Casebook*, the most comprehensive chronicle of Sasquatch sightings from 1818 to 2004, the 1970s remains the peak decade for Bigfoot sightings. In reality Bigfoot never progressed past the 1970s. Almost everybody at the Sasquatch Summit I attended in 2019 was old. If Bigfoot was over sixty and got his hands on a flannel shirt he would have fit right in.

Dr. Robert Michael Pyle, an American lepidopterist who attended a similar Bigfoot convention, famously noted about the attendees "these guys don't want to *find* Bigfoot—they want to *be* Bigfoot." In his unreadably flowery book *Where Bigfoot Walks: Crossing the Dark Divide*, Dr. Pyle comes to the same conclusion as most cultural historians: that Bigfoot represents a link back to nature. The only problem is that Dr. Pyle is a product of the 1960s and has a white 1960s view of nature. Most of his book on Bigfoot is just him jerking off about the beauty of trees. Here is an actual passage from his book about Bigfoot: "Autumn regalia of yellows and reds draped the black cottonwoods, big leaf maples, dogwoods of the Cascade foothills. Vine maples burned candy-apple red, and the cascaras were hung with lemon drops." Now imagine a hundred pages of that. Still, Dr. Pyle is correct in saying that Bigfoot is symptomatic of the white desire for a kindly relationship with the natural world.

Stories of Bigfoot attacking people are regarded as "Hollywood" inventions by those in the Bigfoot community who have been kindly carried back to their porch or cared for by the creature. It should be noted that whites who prefer the "kindly" Bigfoot usually imagine him with red or brown hair and lighter skin. An online illustration for the 2019 Sasquatch Spiritual Retreat in Chewelah, Washington even depicts a peaceful, white Bigfoot with blonde hair in a nordic braid. Whenever someone is confronted by a violent or "evil" Bigfoot, they are depicted as black.

This is even true with Bigfoot movies: *Harry and the Hendersons* (1987), *Big and Hairy* (1998), *The Son of Bigfoot* (2017), *The Missing*

Link (2019), and *Abominable* (2019) all show light haired light skinned Bigfoot helping people. *The Untold* (2002), *Sasquatch Mountain* (2006), and *Bigfoot* (2012) all show a black Sasquatch on the attack.

The racial aspects of interest in Bigfoot have been noted since the 1970s, with the cartoonist Robert Crumb drawing Sasquatch as the attractive black woman "Sassy." The cultural historian Joshua Blu Buhs even went so far as to claim, "By imagining themselves into the body of Sasquatch, white working-class men could imagine themselves as black, as women, could come in contact with their own souls, their own repressed and forbidden desires." I love a good tangent more than anybody, but even I think Buhs started making some weird generalizations in his work on Bigfoot.

To really get why Northwest Baby Boomers were so into Sasquatch in the 1970s we need to take a look at Seattle's Woodland Park Zoo and its revolutionarily innovative gorilla exhibit.

REAL SEATTLE APES

*I*n the post-War years, when Bigfoot reached his highest popularity, the biggest celebrity in Seattle was a western lowland gorilla named Bobo. Anybody born on the Puget Sound from the 1950s to the early 1960s will remember Bobo.

Born in the jungles of Africa, visitors expected Bobo to be an ultra-virile King Kong type monstrous ape. When a female gorilla was brought to him, biologists all over the world were perplexed by the fact that they would not mate. For some reason Bobo did not have any interest in sex. Bill Cosby even did a retroactively creepy stand-up routine about it.

When Bobo died in 1968, an autopsy revealed that he was actually intersex, having an extra X chromosome. He was stuffed standing up, to reflect how on account of being raised by humans his personality was always a mix of both man and ape as well as male and female.

A few weeks before his death, two orangutan twins were born in the Woodland Park Zoo. If Bigfoot doesn't exist, and never existed, the twin orangutans, Towan and Chinta, are the first non-human apes ever born on Puget Sound. Unlike Bobo, the twins proved to be *too* amorous for zoo visitors. Their incestuous relationship was yet another reminder that you can't force human norms onto wild animals. Still, every day hundreds of families would visit the Woodland Park Zoo and would impose western-style nuclear family roles onto wild apes. "Look at the mommy and daddy orangutan!"

The female twin, Chinta, gave birth to a son-nephew, Brute, but he was quietly removed from the zoo and it is not clear what became of him. Until Chinta's death in 2020, the Zoo website claimed that she had no children and her Seattle Times obituary made no mention of him.

A big aspect of the Bigfoot myth is that when real apes don't live up to some fantasy of what nature represents, Bigfoot can still be whatever you want him to be.

In the 1970s, the Woodland Park Zoo was the first zoo in world history to create "landscape immersion." The concept was to put plants and water features in with the animals in order to replicate their natural habitat as much as possible. Jon Coe, one of the planning team members, described the plan's goal was to help visitors understand "we don't own the Earth, the Earth owns us."

Every other zoo on Earth thought this idea was insane, but nobody wants to merge with nature like a Seattleite, and the city loved the idea. The zoo's director at the time, David Hancocks, had a special affinity for apes, a gorilla named Guy at the London

Zoo being what got him interested in zoo architecture in the first place. "It wasn't his huge form that astonished me so much as the intelligence in his eyes." The other thing that astonished Hancocks was the tiny cage Guy was kept in, "no bigger than a garden shed." The floors of the cage were covered in Guy's own feces. Hancocks walked away from that zoo "as I have many others since, feeling confused and depressed."

Naturally, the first exhibit to get an immersive landscape at Woodland Park was the gorilla exhibit. When Kiki, the 450-pound virile gorilla who replaced Bobo, touched grass for the first time he flinched and pulled back. Hancocks observed that Kiki actually started sweating when he saw trees for the first time and flinched once more when a crow flew by, having never seen a bird before.

The new gorilla exhibit made history all over the world for its lifelike depiction of the wild. The famous primatologist Dian Fossey declared that only Seattle's zoo was fit to house gorillas. When she left photos of the exhibit on her desk she came back to find some of her field biology students puzzling over them, trying to figure out where in Africa they'd been taken.

One individual not fooled, however, was Kiki, the 450-pound gorilla. Now that he had some room to think, the zoo staff quickly learned he was much brighter than they had previously thought. Everyday when let out of the cell he was kept in while they cleaned the exhibit, he would always instantly find where they hid his favorite foods, which they scattered around to replicate foraging practices in the wild. After examining his cell they found that from an oblique angle he could watch the security camera and see where his food was hidden, meaning he also knew the places they could watch him.

After he got his food he would spend all day climbing the largest tree in the exhibit, looking out past fake Africa to the real Northwest with its lakes and mountains.

Eventually Kiki decided he wanted to see some of these places for himself. After finding a spot that wasn't covered by the security cameras, he ripped a tree out by the roots and used it as a bridge to cross the moat.

Upon escaping, he quickly realized that he stuck out more than he thought. When he'd been firmly behind a barrier, people liked him. Now that Kiki had crossed the barrier, he became a threat. According to zoo director Hancocks, Kiki sat behind a shrub and "tried to make himself as inconspicuous as possible, which was not very."

Soon visitors were at the administration building complaining that a gorilla was walking around among the public. The staff thought they were confused by the landscape-immersion. They tried explaining that it only looked like a gorilla was among them but it was behind a plate of glass. Then the visitor mentioned the gorilla was on the sidewalk.

Kiki was quickly shot up with tranquilizer darts and hauled back to fake Africa. He woke up in a cell. When he was eventually released back into his landscape-immersion exhibit he found the staff had placed an electric wire across the moat wall. He touched it once, got shocked, and never tried to escape again. The electric wire was invisible to visitors, so the illusion of happy gorillas in their native habitat was maintained.

That day he learned more about Seattle philosophy than many professors of Northwest history ever learn in a lifetime. For all their talk of "we don't own the Earth, the Earth owns us," they very much owned Kiki. Despite replacing bars with glass and putting some grass in his enclosure, he was still their prisoner, not their partner.

For the remainder of the 1970s, when Bigfoot was at the peak of his popularity, Kiki must have seen a visitor in a Bigfoot t-shirt. The image of a thing part-man, part-ape walking upright, free, moving where it pleased through a mythic forest. He knew something about it they didn't.

That it only exists on a t-shirt.

A Bigfoot Hiking Guide

MOUNT ST. HELENS

*B*efore the big 1980 volcanic eruption, St. Helens was *the* Bigfoot capital. It was where Fred Beck first shot one back in 1924 and it is rumored that the U.S. Government airlifted out dozens of Bigfoot carcasses after the 1980 eruption.

While much of the landscape has changed since Fred Beck's time, it's best to start your hike at Ape Canyon where it all started almost 100 years ago. To get to Ape Canyon, it's best to start out in the Bigfoot loving town of Cougar, Washington. It's a great place to get a Bigfoot t-shirt before starting the scenic two and a half hour drive alongside Swift Reservoir and through the Gifford Pinchot National Forest.

Down in the gorge, things are so dusty it's easy to see how a dog could be mistaken for Bigfoot. From the top of the gorge you are surrounded by so many wild flowers, mountain views, and even the wandering mountain goat that you realize the reason they still haven't caught Bigfoot is because how good everything else looks is too distracting.

The whole trail is 11 miles roundtrip and fine for the inexperienced hiker.

If you're at St. Helens with kids, the best place to search for Bigfoot is the Trail of Two Forests. The trail gets its name from the fact that it is two forests in one. The first forest is made of living trees including northwest favorites like the Douglas fir. The other forest is actually made of lava.

1,900 years ago a lava flow flowed through the forest, completely incinerating the trees but leaving impressions of them. Some of the tree molds have formed tiny caves that kids love to crawl through.

It is an overlooked location for Bigfoot hunting, but if the lava made an impression from the trees, what else might it have left an impression of?

If you enjoyed crawling around in the lava tree caves of the Trail of Two Forests, you might like to try the bigger cave, Ape Cave.

Unlike Ape Canyon, Ape Cave is regrettably not named after a Bigfoot sighting. Still, you will not find a better hiding place for a Bigfoot on the mountain.

The third longest lava tube in North America, Ape Cave stretches two miles into the earth. There is a well tended visitor path, but you have to bring your own flashlight as the cave winds into total darkness. Bats hibernate in the cave, although I personally know people paranoid enough to actually believe the bat sounds they hear are really "Batsquatch" the infamous flying Bigfoot spotted flying around Mount St. Helens in the early 1990s.

Other creatures to look out for: mountain goats, black bears, and cougars.

WYNOOCHEE LAKE SHORE TRAIL

*V*isiting the Olympic Peninsula is not only a great place for searching for Bigfoot, but it is a great way to fully understand the story of John Tornow (see chapter 2). As soon as you cross the mountains you'll find yourself in an unending curtain of ocean rain. The landscape is covered in forests cut through with farm land, evocative of the end of the frontier environment connected to the murders.

Wynoochee Lake Shore trail is a great Bigfoot location as any fans of the Animal Planet show *Finding Bigfoot* will know. This was where some great footprints were found back in 2012 and a rather convincing audio recording was made.

It is a great trail to think about the blurred lines between the natural and the artificial. Walking along the trail feels like being in an ancient forest surrounding a lake carved by a glacier, but the local trail was intentionally designed. Wynoochee Lake did not exist until the construction of the Wynoochee Dam in 1972. All the trees are second-growth, planted by logging companies after all the original trees were mowed down.

However, the Wynoochee River that feeds into the lake has been here forever. It was on these shores that John Tornow prowled for victims, and Sasquatch potentially fished for salmon. It almost makes one wonder if they ever saw each other.

Other creatures to look out for: blue heron, bobcats, and the rare spotted owl.

DEVIL'S PUNCHBOWL IN SIX RIVERS NATIONAL FOREST

*T*he wilderness of Humboldt County, California looks like the cover of a Bigfoot book, so it makes sense that there is a Bigfoot inside it somewhere. This is where Roger Patterson made his famous Bigfoot film back in 1967 and thousands of people have been trying to film a sequel ever since.

If there is a Bigfoot left in Humboldt County there is no better place for him than Six Rivers National Forest. Part of the Bigfoot

Trail (an enormous informal hiking trail that goes all the way from Southern Oregon to the middle of California), Six Rivers contains 366 miles of woods, meaning there are plenty of trees for Bigfoot to lurk behind.

There are so many sightings here that it seems like you could basically walk in any direction and see a Bigfoot, but if you're looking for something to make your hike worthwhile in the off chance you don't see one, head to Devil's Punchbowl (not to be confused with the Devil's Punchbowl on the Oregon coast).

High up in the Klamath Mountains, Devil's Punchbowl is a glacial lake of water so clear it looks like somebody just stretched a layer of cling-wrap over the surface. The bowl of mountains surrounding the lake completely blocks out the horizon, making you feel like the world consists of nothing but you, the trees, and the rainbow trout.

After your hike, the town of Willow Creek, California is a short car ride away. A rural community that contains more corny Bigfoot merchandise than people, Willow Creek hosts an annual "Bigfoot Daze" celebration that no Bigfoot fan should miss.

Other creatures to look out for: peregrine falcon, grizzly bears, and salamanders.

MOUNT HOOD NATIONAL FOREST

*M*ount Hood has more Bigfoot sightings than anywhere else in Oregon, which is saying a lot because Oregon is one of the top three Bigfoot sighting states. Bigfoots are so common here that it is where the North American Bigfoot Center has made its home, complete with museum.

For a family accessible hike, go with Tamanawas Falls. "Tamanawas" is a Chinook word that means anything to do with the supernatural. Behind the falls is a dry cave, which hundreds of years ago would have been an ideal burrow for a Bigfoot, but is now eternally filled with hikers eating lunch. The hiking path is usually crowded, but well-cleared, making it great for kids or inexperienced hikers. Best to go early in the morning to avoid the crowds and have a better chance of seeing Bigfoot.

Other creatures to look out for: yellow-bellied marmots, coyotes, and mountain lions.